7/20   1-

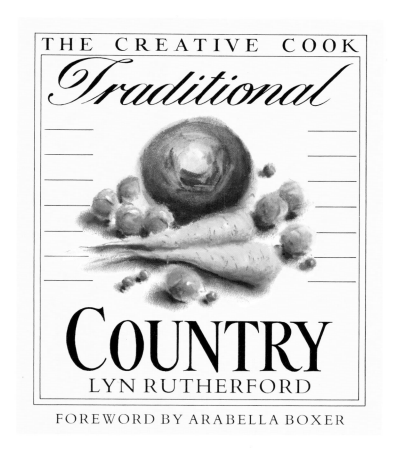

THE CREATIVE COOK

Traditional

COUNTRY

LYN RUTHERFORD

FOREWORD BY ARABELLA BOXER

PHOTOGRAPHY BY DEBBIE PATTERSON

CONRAN OCTOPUS

To my lovely Mother and to Jess, a true friend.

Please note the following:

Quantities given in all the recipes serve 4 people unless otherwise stated.

Spoon measurements are level unless otherwise stated.

Metric and imperial measures are both given, use one or the other as the two are not interchangeable.

Flour used is plain white flour, unless otherwise specified.

Preparation of ingredients, such as the cleaning, trimming and peeling of vegetables and fruit, is presumed and the text only refers to any aspect of this if unusual, such as onions used unpeeled etc.

Citrus fruit is generally coated in a layer of preservative wax. For this reason, whenever a recipe uses the rind of oranges, lemons or limes the text specifies unwaxed fruit. If organic uncoated fruit is not available, scrub the fruit vigorously in hot soapy water, rinse well and pat dry.

Eggs used are size 3 (65 g/2¼ oz) unless otherwise specified. The Government recommends that eggs not be consumed raw, and people most at risk, such as children, old people, invalids and pregnant women, should not eat them lightly cooked. This book includes recipes with raw and lightly cooked eggs, which should not be eaten by the above categories. These recipes are marked by a * in the text. Once prepared, these dishes should be kept refrigerated and used promptly.

Editorial Direction: Lewis Esson Publishing
Art Director: Mary Evans
Design: Sue Storey
Illustrations: Alison Barratt
Food for Photography: Lyn Rutherford
Styling: Sue Skeen
Editorial Assistant: Penny David
Production: Jill Macey

First published in 1992 by
Conran Octopus Limited,
37 Shelton Street, London WC2H 9HN

British Library Cataloguing in
Publication Data
A catalogue record for this book is available from the
British Library

ISBN 1-85029-434-8

Typeset by Hunters Armley Ltd
Printed and bound by Arnoldo Mondadori Editore,
Verona

CONTENTS

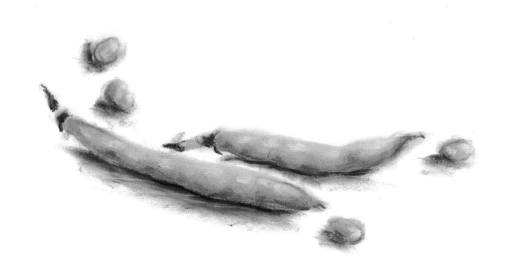

FOREWORD

Traditional country dishes have been the backbone of my cooking and eating ever since I left school forty years ago to become master of my own destiny – at least in the kitchen. This is the food that I have relied on for sustenance and pleasure alike, to feed my family and entertain my friends. It is not exclusively British, for the cuisines of the Mediterranean and North Africa, the Middle East, India and North America are in some ways more suited to our needs today than a purely British diet. With our current enthusiasm for lighter dishes which are low in cholesterol and animal fats, some of the ethnic foods offer a healthy alternative to our native fare.

Many of the dishes in this book are truly traditional: classics like soused herrings, steak and mushroom pudding, and crème brûlée. Others have an added twist, reminding us that the title of the series is *The Creative Cook*. Thus kedgeree is flavoured with whole coriander seeds – an unusual but welcome innovation, referring back to its Indian origins – and the fish cakes are accompanied by a dill and egg sauce, giving a Scandinavian touch to an old English favourite.

In recent years I have grown aware of two distinct trends in British food. On the one hand we have the modern cuisine of the innovative chefs: stylish dishes to be enjoyed as an occasional treat in a first-rate restaurant, or in the home of an inspired amateur. These dishes rarely become familiar, for they are changing constantly. Much of their appeal lies in their novelty, and by the time one revisits the restaurant – or the friend's house – they have moved on to other things. On the other hand we have our traditional country fare, as depicted in this book. This is what I call 'real food', and this is what I prefer to cook for the mainstream of family and social life. For it is in this sort of food that we find embodied the solid values of home, the comfort of the family and a reassuring sense of familiarity.

ARABELLA BOXER

INTRODUCTION

*T*he traditional country food explored in this book by no means consists entirely of British dishes. I have deliberately included classic favourites from rural Europe and America – the unifying feature being that all the recipes are for good plain local food as enjoyed by many generations of countryfolk.

The recipes are thus characterized by their clever and economic use of simple seasonal ingredients. There is no hint here of trendy restaurant dishes or of the considerations of 'fast' and 'convenience' food. Instead you will find timeless good food, full of reassuringly familiar flavours.

In the spirit of the *Creative Cook* series, as well as giving a selection of expected favourites I have also tried to give a fresh look to some of the more conventional dishes.

Left: an apple and nectarine variation of Apple and Berry Crumble (page 61); right: Spiced Golden Squash Soup (page 12)

My recipes bring in a little of our modern adventurousness and facility with exotic spices, fruits and vegetables and give the food a lighter, healthier slant – after all, most of us nowadays no longer expend our energy on a day's heavy physical labour.

More than anything else, traditional country food had the very definite purpose of satisfying hungry toilers on their return from the fields. For this reason it is unashamedly filling, warming and sustaining. This wholesomeness gives it a very broad appeal – to everyone from those who crave the comfort of nursery foods, like creamy rice and steamed puddings, to the health-conscious concerned with a more natural diet.

In most rural homes, the kitchen was the heart of the house and the stove produced all the warmth and hot water for the entire household as well as the family meals. The dictates of such requirements meant that food was usually cooked by long slow methods, like stewing, braising, roasting and baking, often with two or three dishes cooking together. Bread was baked in the morning, while pastries, cakes and puddings occupied the oven in the early afternoon, to leave plenty of time for the dishes of the evening meal to be cooked ready for the homecoming of the hungry workers back from the fields.

Ingredients used were mostly local home-grown produce. Even the humblest of cottages would have a fairly substantial vegetable garden and many supported a few chickens or geese – or even a pig or two. The shrewd ways of the country also meant that much was made of the range of wild and freely available foodstuffs, from hedgerow herbs and forest mushrooms to small game like rabbits and birds.

Fishing was also more than a recreational pastime for most countryfolk. Those on the coast would have their own crab and lobster pots and perhaps even a small boat and some nets for making the most of the bounty of the sea. Inland, fish like brown trout, salmon and carp were caught by rod and line – or even by hand! – as regular treats. Even tasty crayfish were abundant in mountain streams.

Because of the seasonal nature of such food supplies, rural cooks became masters of the various methods of food preservation. Country kitchens became tireless hives of industry whenever there was a glut of any item, be it the making of jams and preserves from summer fruits, the salting in deep crocks of a good vegetable harvest or the smoking of an abundance of fish or seafood.

Those families which kept a cow or some goats also became skilled in making a wide range of dairy products. As well as producing their own daily supplies of butter and cream, many households would make their own simple cheeses as a means of keeping the goodness of the summer pastures to give pleasure and nourishment in the darkest days of winter.

In many parts of the world, the annual slaughtering of the household pig became a festive occasion. Families – or even entire neighbourhoods –

would come together to enjoy a celebratory roast joint cooked on a spit over an open fire, while the rest of the beast was put to an amazingly ingenious range of uses, from being cured into hams and bacon to becoming incorporated into sausages both fresh and dried, like the extraordinary variety of French charcuterie and Italian salami.

Nothing would go to waste. Even the trotters would be stuffed as a special treat and the tasty skin made into irresistible crisp pork 'scratchings'. These pork products would not only continue to supply the family with meat and protein throughout the rest of the year, but they would also provide an invaluable source of extra flavouring for all manner of dishes, from simple soups and stews to stuffing mixtures, pâtés and terrines.

For it was – and still is – flavour which forms the essence of traditional country food. Tried and tested combinations of fresh tasty ingredients are cooked in a sympathetic manner in order to bring out the depth of their flavours to the fullest. Nowadays we all of us have less time to spend in the kitchen preparing our meals, but this does not necessarily mean that we have to make do with packaged convenience food or miss out on good old-fashioned wholesomeness and flavour.

Traditional dishes are often, by necessity, very simple to prepare. Stocks, stews and steamed puddings can involve only a handful of ingredients and the minimum of preparation – and may be left virtually to cook themselves. Nowadays, with the help of invaluable gadgets like food processors and automatic ovens – and dishwashers! – even baking can involve the minimum of time actually spent in the kitchen. All that is really needed is more of the invaluable – ancient and modern – skill of forward planning.

Many of the recipes in this book lend themselves very well to today's busy lifestyles, as they may easily be adapted to allow their preparation in easy stages. For instance, pie fillings – both sweet and savoury – may be simmered well in advance (perhaps even frozen in batches) and then baked with freshly made short buttery golden pastry while the rest of the meal is being prepared. Moreover, a lot of traditional fare – especially soups, stews and casseroles – actually tastes all the better for having been made ahead of time and then allowed to stand for a day or two before being reheated, as this gives the constituent flavours an opportunity to develop more fully and to intermingle. Many families grew up looking forward eagerly to their brimming bowls of 'second-day's soup'.

It is this eternal image of families sitting down together in the happy anticipation of the joys of plain simple food that really encapsulates for me the feeling of traditional country food. My hope is that using the recipes which follow in this book will allow you too perhaps to enjoy with your family a wide variety of home-made food which is neither very complicated nor all that expensive, which is made from readily obtained ingredients, and which – above all – provides both nourishment and deep satisfaction.

SOUPS

Hearty nourishing soups are central to traditional cooking. With good tasty stock constantly simmering on the stove and a ready supply of fresh vegetables, herbs and other ingredients, most country meals feature a substantial bowl of soup. In the farmhouse tradition, as well as performing their more usual role as first courses and as lunches – served with lots of fresh crusty bread – many of the soups in this chapter may also be readily adapted to make meals in themselves. The broth may be served as a first course and then the remaining ingredients served as a main course or, as with *Crab Gumbo*, the entire dish may be served accompanied by rice or potatoes.

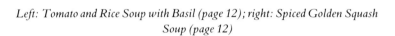

Left: Tomato and Rice Soup with Basil (page 12); right: Spiced Golden Squash Soup (page 12)

The BUTTERNUT SQUASH *is the distinctively peanut-shaped, pale yellowy-orange variety of winter squash. If unavailable, any hard-skinned squash or pumpkin will work in this recipe.*

SPICED GOLDEN SQUASH SOUP

SERVES 6

900 g/2 lb butternut squash
55 g/2 oz butter
white parts only of 4 leeks, thinly sliced
1 tbsp coriander seeds, crushed
large pinch of ground allspice
large pinch of freshly grated nutmeg
700 ml/1¼ pt chicken stock
300 ml/½ pt milk
salt and freshly ground black pepper
6 tbsp single cream, to garnish

Peel the squash, cut the flesh into 2.5 cm/1 in cubes and discard the seeds.

Melt the butter in a large saucepan over a moderate heat. Add the leeks and cook, stirring, for 5-6 minutes until they are soft and beginning to colour. Stir in the squash, coriander seeds, allspice and nutmeg and cook for 1 minute.

Stir in the stock, season with salt and pepper and bring to the boil. Cover and simmer for about 35 minutes, until the squash is very soft.

Purée the soup, in batches, using a blender or food processor. Return the puréed soup to the pan and stir in the milk. Reheat gently and adjust the seasoning to taste.

Serve garnished with swirls of cream.

TOMATO AND RICE SOUP WITH BASIL

SERVES 4–6

1 tbsp olive oil
1 large onion, finely chopped
1 garlic clove, crushed
1 small red sweet pepper, deseeded and chopped
45 g/1½ oz Milano or other Italian salami, chopped
900 g/2 lb ripe tomatoes, peeled, deseeded and chopped
1 tbsp tomato paste
sprig of oregano
200 ml/7 fl oz dry white wine
575 ml/1 pt chicken or vegetable stock
45 g/1½ oz risotto rice, preferably arborio
3 tbsp chopped basil
salt and freshly ground black pepper
bread sticks or crusty Italian bread, to serve

Heat the oil in a large heavy-based saucepan over a moderate heat, add the onion and garlic and cook for 5 minutes, without browning. Stir in the red pepper and salami and cook for 2 minutes.

Add the tomatoes, tomato paste and oregano and stir in the wine and stock. Season, bring to the boil then lower the heat, cover and simmer for 20 minutes.

Add the rice and basil to the pan, cover and continue cooking for 15 minutes, until the rice is tender.

Serve accompanied by bread sticks or crusty Italian bread.

CREAM OF MUSHROOM SOUP WITH MARSALA

45 g/1½ oz butter
675 g/1½ lb mushrooms, roughly chopped
1 shallot, finely chopped
½ garlic clove, chopped
2 tbsp flour
100 ml/3½ fl oz Marsala
700 ml/1¼ pt well-flavoured chicken or vegetable stock
175 ml/6 fl oz double cream
salt and freshly ground black pepper
chopped flat-leaf parsley or chervil, to garnish

Melt the butter in a large heavy-based saucepan. Add the mushrooms, shallots and garlic and cook, stirring, for 4 minutes.

Stir in the flour and continue cooking for 1 minute. Gradually stir in the Marsala and stock. Season and bring to the boil. Then lower the heat, cover and simmer for 20 minutes.

Purée the soup in a blender or food processor, in batches if necessary, until smooth and then return it to the pan.

Just before serving, stir in all but 4 tablespoons of the cream and heat the soup through gently. Adjust the seasoning and serve garnished with swirls of the reserved cream and the parsley or chervil.

Note: if available, field mushrooms will give a much better flavour than cultivated ones. A mixture of mushroom varieties is best, particularly if it includes a few ceps.

BORSCHT

SERVES 6

350 g/12 oz cooked beetroot, peeled and grated
2 carrots, grated
1 onion, finely chopped
1 celery stalk, finely chopped
850 ml/1½ pt beef stock
strip of zest and 1 tbsp juice from an unwaxed lemon
bouquet garni
175 ml/6 fl oz sour cream
salt and freshly ground black pepper

Put the beetroot in a large pan with the carrots, onion and celery. Stir in the stock, lemon zest and bouquet garni. Season with salt and pepper. Bring to the boil then lower the heat, cover and simmer for 40 minutes.

Remove the lemon zest and bouquet garni. Purée the soup, in batches, using a blender or food processor. Strain into a bowl or serving tureen and leave to cool.

When the soup is completely cold, stir in the lemon juice and all but 6 tablespoons of the sour cream. Adjust the seasoning to taste. Cover and chill for at least 2 hours.

Swirl the reserved sour cream into the soup to serve.

Versions of BORSCHT, or beetroot soup, are traditional throughout Eastern Europe, especially in Poland and Russia. The soup may be served either hot or cold, with sour cream swirled into it.

SCOTCH BROTH

SERVES 6

450 g/1 lb neck fillet of lamb, trimmed of fat and cut into
2 or 3 pieces
55 g/2 oz pearl barley
850 ml/1½ pt well-flavoured beef or lamb stock
bouquet garni
4 celery stalks, sliced
225 g/8 oz carrots, sliced
3 leeks, sliced
1 small swede, diced
170 g/6 oz potato, diced
1 large onion, chopped
100 ml/3½ fl oz dry sherry (optional)
salt and freshly ground black pepper

Put the meat in a large pan together with the pearl barley, stock and bouquet garni. Season with salt and pepper. Bring to the boil and carefully skim off any scum.

Lower the heat, cover and simmer for 1¼ hours, skimming occasionally. Use paper towels to soak up the excess fat on the surface.

Remove the meat from the pan and set it aside. Add the vegetables to the pan. Bring the soup back to the boil, then cover and simmer for about 30 minutes.

Cut the meat into small pieces and add these back to the pan with the dry sherry, if using. Simmer for a further 10-15 minutes and adjust the seasoning before serving.

Note: make a chicken broth, replacing the lamb with a large boiling fowl and the stock with water.

MINESTRONE SOUP

SERVES 6–8

170 g/6 oz piece of unsmoked bacon, chopped
1 large onion, finely chopped
1 garlic clove, crushed
3 carrots, diced
3 celery stalks, thinly sliced
225 g/8 oz potatoes, diced
450 g/1 lb tomatoes, peeled and chopped
*170 g/6 oz dried cannellini beans, soaked overnight
in cold water*
1.1 litre/2 pt stock or water
½ small white cabbage, finely shredded
2 courgettes, thinly sliced
170 g/6 oz fresh or frozen garden peas
140 g/5 oz macaroni or other small pasta
2 tbsp chopped flat-leaf parsley
handful of basil leaves, shredded
salt and freshly ground black pepper
6–8 tbsp freshly grated Parmesan cheese, to serve

Put the bacon in a large heavy-based saucepan over a moderate heat and cook for a few minutes until the fat begins to melt. Add the onion and cook for about 5 minutes more until that is soft.

Stir in the garlic, carrots, celery, potatoes, tomatoes and drained beans. Pour in the stock and bring to the boil. Lower the heat, cover and simmer for about 2 hours, until the beans are tender.

Add the cabbage, courgettes, peas, macaroni and parsley to the pan, cover and cook for a further 20 minutes.

Just before serving, stir in the basil and season with salt and pepper. Serve piping hot, sprinkled with freshly grated Parmesan.

Clockwise from the top centre: Minestrone Soup, Lentil and Ham Soup (page 18) and Cream of Mushroom Soup with Marsala (page 13)

SPRING CHICKEN AND LEEK SOUP

5 tbsp olive oil
1 large onion, chopped
2 bay leaves
sprig of thyme
2 dressed poussins, each weighing about 450 g/1 lb
150 ml/¼ pt dry white wine
450 g/1 lb leeks, diced
115 g/4 oz potatoes, diced
large pinch of freshly grated nutmeg
150 ml/¼ pt double cream
salt and freshly ground black pepper

Heat 2 tablespoons of the oil in a large heavy-based saucepan over a moderate heat, add the onion and cook, stirring, for about 10 minutes until it is pale golden in colour.

Add the bay leaves, thyme and poussins to the pan and pour over the wine. Add just enough water to cover the birds (about 850 ml/1½ pt). Bring to the boil then lower the heat, cover and simmer for 30–40 minutes, until the poussins are cooked.

Remove the birds from the stock and set aside until cool enough to handle. Strain the stock into a large bowl, discarding the herbs and onion.

Heat the remaining oil in the saucepan. Add the leeks and potatoes and sauté for 2–3 minutes. Pour over the reserved stock and bring to the boil. Season with freshly grated nutmeg, salt and pepper. Cover and simmer for 25–30 minutes, stirring occasionally.

Meanwhile, remove the flesh from the poussins, cut it into dice or strips and add these to the soup.

Just before serving, stir the cream into the soup and warm through gently. Adjust the seasoning to taste, if necessary.

The exact recipe for MINESTRONE, *the classic vegetable soup of Italy, varies from region to region. Generally, however, it is garnished with pasta and sprinkled with grated Parmesan cheese.*

LENTIL AND HAM SOUP WITH MUSHROOM TOASTS

SERVES 6

30 g/1 oz butter
1 large onion, chopped
1 garlic clove, crushed
1 carrot, finely diced
1 celery stalk, finely diced
350 g/12 oz red lentils
1 bay leaf
sprig of thyme
1 tbsp chopped parsley (optional)
salt and freshly ground black pepper
FOR THE HAM STOCK
1 smoked ham joint, weighing about 675 g/1½ lb
1 onion, quartered
1 carrot, quartered
6 black peppercorns
FOR THE MUSHROOM TOASTS
45 g/1½ oz butter
55 g/2 oz mushrooms, finely chopped
2 tsp chopped parsley
½ garlic clove, crushed
6 small slices of French bread

The MUSHROOM TOASTS *make good starters or snacks on their own. Just double or triple the quantities, depending on appetites.*

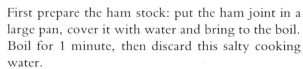

First prepare the ham stock: put the ham joint in a large pan, cover it with water and bring to the boil. Boil for 1 minute, then discard this salty cooking water.

Add 1.5 litre/2½ pt of fresh cold water to the pan with the onion, carrot and peppercorns. Return to the boil, then lower the heat, cover and simmer for about 1½ hours, until the ham is tender.

Transfer the ham to a plate and leave to cool. Then cut it into small dice or flake it with a fork and set aside. Leave the stock to cool, then remove the fat which rises to the surface. Strain the stock and reserve.

Melt the butter in a large saucepan over a moderate heat. Add the onion, garlic, carrot and celery and cook, stirring, for 3-4 minutes. Stir in the lentils, bay leaf and thyme and add the reserved ham stock. Bring to the boil then lower the heat, cover and simmer for 1-1½ hours.

About 10 minutes before serving, make the mushroom toasts: first preheat a hot grill.

Melt the butter in a small heavy-based pan over a moderate to high heat. Add the mushrooms, parsley and garlic and cook, stirring frequently, until all the liquid which exudes from the mushrooms is evaporated. Season with salt and pepper.

Toast the bread slices on one side under the grill. Then turn them over and divide the mushroom mixture between them. Return them to the grill for 1 minute only, until well heated through.

Season the soup with salt and pepper. Remove and discard the bay and thyme and stir in the parsley, if using. Serve piping hot, accompanied by the mushroom toasts.

CRAB GUMBO

225 g/8 oz crab meat plus 4 crab claws
450 g/1 lb raw king prawns
45 g/1½ oz butter
170 g/6 oz okra, halved
1 onion, chopped
2 garlic cloves, finely chopped
1 celery stalk, chopped
1 small green sweet pepper, deseeded and chopped
170 g/6 oz pumpkin, peeled and diced
2 tbsp flour
3 tomatoes, peeled and coarsely chopped
2 bay leaves
sprig of thyme
1 tbsp chopped parsley
1 tbsp Worcestershire sauce
hot pepper sauce to taste
salt and freshly ground black pepper

Shell the crab claws. Shell and devein the prawns. Put all the shells in a pan, cover with 1.1 litre/2 pt of water and bring to the boil. Cover and simmer gently for 30 minutes. Strain, reserving the stock.

Melt half the butter in a large heavy-based pan over a moderate heat. Add the okra and cook for 3 minutes. Stir in the onion, garlic, celery and sweet pepper and cook, stirring, for about 4 minutes, until softened. Add the pumpkin and cook for 1 minute. Transfer to a bowl or plate and set aside.

Melt the remaining butter in the pan and stir in the flour. Cook for 3-4 minutes, until it is beginning to brown. Add the tomatoes and gradually stir in the reserved fish stock.

Add the reserved vegetables with the herbs, Worcestershire sauce and hot pepper sauce to taste. Bring to the boil, stirring, until thick. Simmer for 20 minutes, then stir in the prawns and crab meat and cook for 10 minutes more. Adjust the seasoning and add more pepper sauce, if necessary.

FISH CHOWDER

SERVES 4–6

450 g/1 lb cod or haddock fillets
3 slices of unsmoked bacon, rinds removed and chopped
30 g/1 oz butter
1 large onion, chopped
1 bay leaf
large pinch of saffron strands
450 g/1 lb potatoes, peeled and diced
2 tomatoes, peeled, deseeded and chopped
2 tbsp snipped chives
2 tbsp chopped parsley
300 ml/½ pt single cream
170 g/6 oz peeled cooked prawns
salt and freshly ground black pepper
warm crusty bread, to serve

Put the fish in a large shallow pan with the bacon. Pour over 850 ml/1½ pt of water and bring to the boil. Lower the heat, cover and then simmer gently for 8-10 minutes, until the fish flakes readily.

Transfer the fish to a plate and allow it to cool. Strain the liquid and reserve. When the fish is cool enough to handle, skin and flake the flesh into large bite-sized pieces, removing any bones. Set aside.

Melt the butter in a large heavy-based saucepan over a moderate heat. Add the onion, bay leaf and saffron and cook for 8-10 minutes, stirring frequently, until the onion is soft and a rich golden colour.

Stir in the potatoes and reserved fish stock. Cook for 10-15 minutes, stirring frequently, until the potatoes are tender.

Stir in the tomatoes, herbs and cream together with the reserved flaked fish. Bring back to the boil and simmer gently for 3 minutes, then stir in the prawns. Continue cooking for just 2 minutes to warm the soup through.

Serve accompanied by warm crusty bread.

The GUMBO is the glory of Louisiana's Creole cuisine. These thick stews, usually containing shellfish and poultry, are thickened with okra and, traditionally, powdered sassafras leaves.

This CRAB GUMBO serves 4 as a first-course soup, but accompanied by rice or sweet potatoes it can make a meal in itself for 4-6 people.

FISH AND SHELLFISH

*R*ural coastal areas are usually famed for their ingenious ways with seafood, and river fish are a regular treat in most country kitchens. Nowadays shellfish like scallops, mussels, prawns and oysters – and even some fish – are thought of as rather sophisticated ingredients which are the reserve of grand city restaurants. In the old days, of course, their abundance made them poor men's food. This is reflected in the simple manner in which they were traditionally cooked – unadorned with rich creamy sauces flavoured with brandy and truffles. Instead, their delicate flavours are brought out by the addition of readily obtained ingredients such as herbs, cheeses, nuts and fruit.

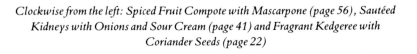

Clockwise from the left: Spiced Fruit Compote with Mascarpone (page 56), Sautéed Kidneys with Onions and Sour Cream (page 41) and Fragrant Kedgeree with Coriander Seeds (page 22)

SKATE *are related to rays and sharks. They are so large that only skinned pieces of the 'wings' are seen in the shops. Thicker pieces give the best value, as the proportion of flesh to skeleton is higher. Skate is the only fish which is better for being a day or two out of the water. It may smell faintly of ammonia, but this is actually a sign of freshness and will go on cooking.*

KEDGEREE *originated in British India and quickly became a favourite breakfast dish back home. The original Indian dish consisted simply of rice with onions and eggs and the British added fish.*

SKATE WITH CAPERS AND BLACK BUTTER

4 pieces of skate, each weighing 225-285 g/8-10 oz, skinned
1 small onion, sliced
1 bay leaf
1 tbsp chopped parsley plus a few parsley stalks
300 ml/½ pt dry white wine (optional)
1½ tbsp capers
55 g/2 oz butter
1 tsp black peppercorns, lightly crushed
2 tbsp white wine vinegar
salt

Place the skate in a large pan with the onion, bay leaf and the parsley stalks. Pour over the white wine, if using, or water to cover. Bring to the boil, then lower the heat and simmer for 12-15 minutes, until the fish is just cooked firm.

Using a fish slice, transfer the fish to a large warmed dish. Sprinkle with the chopped parsley and capers and season with the salt. Cover loosely with foil and keep hot.

Melt the butter in a pan with the peppercorns, allowing the butter to foam and brown slightly. Pour this mixture over the fish. Add the vinegar to the pan and bring to the boil, swirling it around.

Pour the contents of the pan over the fish and serve at once.

FRAGRANT KEDGEREE WITH CORIANDER SEEDS

225 g/8 oz basmati rice
450 g/1 lb smoked cod or haddock
2 bay leaves
1 small onion, halved
1 tbsp coriander seeds, lightly crushed
½ tsp turmeric
300 ml/½ pt milk
30 g/1 oz butter
3 hard-boiled eggs, shelled
salt and freshly ground black pepper
chopped fresh parsley, to garnish (optional)
lemon wedges, to garnish

Cook the rice in 575 ml/1 pt of simmering salted water in a covered pan for 8-10 minutes, until all the water is absorbed. Set aside and keep hot.

Put the fish in a large shallow pan together with the bay leaves, onion and spices. Pour over the milk, bring to the boil and poach gently for 5 minutes.

Remove and discard the onion. Lift out the fish and transfer it to a plate. When it is cool enough to handle, skin and flake the fish, removing any bones. Add the fish flesh to the rice.

Add the butter to the contents of the pan, bring to the boil and cook rapidly for 3 minutes to reduce slightly.

Coarsely chop 2 of the hard-boiled eggs and add these to the pan. Warm through for a minute or so, then add to the reserved rice and fish mixture. Toss lightly to mix.

Season with pepper and serve immediately, sprinkled with chopped fresh parsley, if using, and garnished with lemon wedges and the remaining hard-boiled egg, cut in slices or quarters.

SALMON FISH CAKES WITH DILL AND EGG SAUCE*

450 g/1 lb salmon (tail piece)
150 ml/¼ pt milk
6 black peppercorns
1 bay leaf
225 g/8 oz potatoes, peeled
30 g/1 oz butter
1 egg yolk
*(*see page 2 for advice on eggs)*
1 tsp finely grated zest from an unwaxed lemon
1 tbsp finely chopped parsley
salt and freshly ground black pepper
flour, for dusting
vegetable oil, for frying
FOR THE DILL AND EGG SAUCE
30 g/1 oz butter
150 ml/¼ pt single cream
2 hard-boiled eggs, shelled and chopped
2 tbsp chopped dill
2 tsp lemon juice

Put the salmon, milk, peppercorns and bay leaf in a saucepan. Bring to the boil, cover and then simmer gently for 15 minutes.

Transfer the fish to a plate, reserving the cooking liquid. When cool enough to handle remove and discard the skin. Flake the fish flesh into a large bowl, removing any bones. Mash lightly with a fork.

While the fish is cooking, cut the potatoes into 3.5 cm/1½ in chunks and cook them in boiling salted water for 12-15 minutes until soft. Drain well and return to the heat for a few seconds to dry. Add the butter and 1 tablespoon of the reserved cooking liquid from the fish. Mash until smooth.

Add the potato to the fish together with the egg yolk, lemon zest and parsley. Season with salt and pepper. Mix together lightly, then divide the mixture into 4 equal portions and shape these into

flat cakes on a floured surface. Chill until required.

Meanwhile prepare the sauce: melt the butter in a small pan. Add the cream, hard-boiled eggs and dill and bring to the boil. Cook, stirring, for 2-3 minutes until creamy. Stir in the lemon juice, season and keep warm while cooking the fish cakes.

Heat the oil in a frying pan over a moderate heat. When the oil is quite hot, cook the fish cakes for 6-8 minutes until golden brown, turning once or twice.

Serve the cooked fish cakes with the sauce.

BAKED COD IN CHEESE SAUCE

30 g/1 oz butter
4 cod steaks, each about 2.5 cm/1 in thick
juice of ½ lemon
salt and freshly ground black pepper
FOR THE CHEESE SAUCE
450 ml/¾ pt milk
1 bay leaf
1 small onion, quartered
2 cloves (optional)
30 g/1 oz butter
30 g/1 oz flour
1 tsp Dijon mustard
85 g/3 oz mature farmhouse Cheddar cheese
3 tbsp double cream
large pinch of freshly grated nutmeg
15 g/½ oz fresh white breadcrumbs

Preheat the oven to 180C/350F/gas4 and use a little of the butter to grease a shallow ovenproof dish large enough to hold the cod steaks in one layer.

Arrange the fish in the dish and sprinkle with the lemon juice, salt and pepper. Dot with the remaining butter. Cover loosely with foil and bake in the oven for about 30 minutes, removing the foil after 20 minutes.

Meanwhile, prepare the cheese sauce: put the milk in a small saucepan with the bay leaf, onion and cloves, if using. Bring to the boil, then cover and leave to infuse for 15-20 minutes. Strain.

Melt the butter in another small heavy-based saucepan. Stir in the flour and cook, stirring, for 1-2 minutes. Stir in the mustard. Gradually add the strained milk, stirring constantly. Bring to the boil, still stirring, and cook until thick and smooth.

Left: one of the Salmon Fish Cakes with Dill and Egg Sauce (page 23); right: Baked Cod in Cheese Sauce

Add 55 g/2 oz of the cheese to the sauce and stir until smooth again. Stir in the cream and season with nutmeg, salt and pepper.

Pour the hot sauce over and around the cod steaks. Sprinkle with the breadcrumbs and the remaining cheese. Return to the oven and bake for a further 8-10 minutes until browned.

TROUT WITH ALMONDS

4 whole trout, cleaned
2 tbsp light olive oil
1 shallot, finely chopped
1 garlic clove, crushed
55 g/2 oz flaked almonds
85 g/3 oz butter
grated zest and juice of ½ unwaxed lemon
1 tbsp chopped parsley
salt and freshly ground black pepper
lemon wedges, to garnish
parsley sprigs, to garnish

Preheat a hot grill.

Using a sharp knife, make 2 or 3 diagonal slits into the flesh of each side of the fish. Season the fish inside and out with salt and pepper.

Cook the fish under the grill for about 3 minutes on each side, until the flesh flakes easily from the bone. Do not allow it to overcook or it will be dry.

Meanwhile, heat the oil in a frying pan over a moderate heat. Add the shallot and garlic and cook for 2-3 minutes until soft. Stir in the almonds and cook until they are pale golden in colour.

Add the butter and allow it to sizzle, but take care that it does not burn. Stir in the lemon zest and juice and the chopped parsley. Season to taste.

Transfer the cooked fish to warmed serving plates and spoon over the almond butter mixture. Serve at once, garnished with lemon and parsley.

The TROUT WITH ALMONDS may be made with any type of trout. Farmed rainbow trout are more common and economical, but wild brown trout – when available – are much tastier.

These two recipes are good examples of how oily fish such as mackerel, herrings, sardines – and even salmon – suit sharp dressings that offset their fattiness.

BAKED MACKEREL WITH GOOSEBERRY SAUCE

15 g/½ oz butter
4 whole mackerel, cleaned
4 sprigs of rosemary
1 large onion, thinly sliced
100 ml/3½ fl oz dry white wine
salt and freshly ground black pepper
FOR THE GOOSEBERRY SAUCE
30 g/1 oz butter
1 shallot, finely chopped
450 g/1 lb gooseberries, halved
25 g/¾ oz caster sugar

Preheat the oven to 200C/400F/gas6 and use the butter to grease a shallow ovenproof dish large enough to take the fish in one layer.

Cut the heads from the mackerel, if preferred. Using a sharp knife, make 2 or 3 deep slits into the flesh on each side. Tuck a rosemary sprig into the cavity of each fish and season them inside and out with salt and pepper.

Arrange the onion slices in the base of the baking dish and place the mackerel on top. Pour over the wine and bake for 30 minutes, until the fish is tender and the flesh flakes easily from the bone.

Meanwhile, prepare the gooseberry sauce: melt the butter in a small heavy-based saucepan over a moderate heat. Add the shallot and cook for 4-5 minutes, until soft but not coloured.

Add the gooseberries, sugar and 2 tablespoons of water. Season with salt and pepper. Cover and cook for 10 minutes, stirring frequently, until soft.

Purée the sauce in a blender or food processor and then pass this through a sieve. Return the sieved purée to the pan.

When the mackerel is cooked, add 2-3 tablespoons of the cooking liquid to the sauce and warm it through. Adjust the seasoning to serve.

SOUSED HERRINGS

SERVES 6

12 fresh herrings, cleaned
blade of mace
1 bay leaf
6 black peppercorns
2 cloves
1 onion, sliced
125 ml/4 fl oz white wine vinegar
salt and freshly ground black pepper

Preheat the oven to 200C/400F/gas6.

Remove and discard the heads of the herrings. Cut the fish along the opening made from cleaning them, down to the tail. Lay them skin side up and press firmly along the backbones to loosen them. Turn them over and lift away the bones.

Season the filleted fish with salt and pepper and roll them up to the tail. Secure each rolled herring with a wooden cocktail stick.

Arrange the rolled herrings in a baking dish or roasting pan and add the mace, bay leaf, peppercorns and cloves. Scatter the onion slices over and around the fish. Mix the vinegar with 125 ml/4 fl oz of water and pour this over the fish.

Cover the dish with foil and bake in the oven for about 40 minutes, removing the foil for the last 15 minutes of cooking.

Serve hot with buttered new potatoes, or leave to cool in the baking dish and serve cold with salad and rye bread.

Baked Mackerel with Gooseberry Sauce

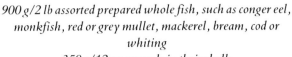

FISH AND SHELLFISH STEW

SERVES 6

900 g/2 lb assorted prepared whole fish, such as conger eel,
monkfish, red or grey mullet, mackerel, bream, cod or
whiting
350 g/12 oz mussels in their shells
2 crab claws, shells broken
225 g/8 oz crayfish or large prawns in their shells
4 tbsp olive oil
1 onion, chopped
1 large leek, sliced
3 garlic cloves, chopped
1 small fennel bulb, sliced
450 g/1 lb ripe tomatoes, peeled and chopped
1 bay leaf
bouquet garni
large pinch of saffron strands
2 strips of zest from an unwaxed orange
300 ml/½ pt dry white wine
salt and freshly ground black pepper
toasted slices of French bread, to serve
chopped fresh parsley, to garnish

Remove the heads and bones from the fish (or get the fishmonger to do it). Set aside the fish and put the trimmings into a large saucepan. Add water to cover and bring to the boil. Then lower the heat, cover and simmer for 15 minutes. Strain and reserve the stock.

Cut the fish into pieces. Scrub the mussels and remove any 'beards'. Discard any open mussels which do not close on being tapped. Rinse the crab claws and the crayfish or prawns.

Heat the oil in a large saucepan over a moderate heat. Add the onion, leek, garlic and fennel and cook gently for 10 minutes, stirring frequently.

Add the tomatoes, herbs, saffron, orange zest and wine to the pan. Pour in the strained fish stock and bring to the boil. Season. Boil for 10 minutes, then lower the heat to a gentle simmer.

Add the fish in batches, starting with firm-fleshed types, such as conger eel and monkfish, which will need up to 10 minutes cooking, followed by the flaky white fish, such as cod and whiting. Finally add the shellfish, which will require only 2 or 3 minutes cooking. Discard any mussels which do not open.

First serve the broth poured into soup bowls over the toasted slices of French bread. Serve the seafood as a separate course, sprinkled with chopped fresh parsley to garnish.

PRAWN AND SCALLOP PIE

675 g/1½ lb potatoes, peeled and quartered
55 g/2 oz butter
6 tbsp single cream
large pinch of freshly grated nutmeg
white parts only of 4 spring onions, chopped
2 tomatoes, peeled, deseeded and quartered
170 g/6 oz oyster mushrooms
450 g/1 lb shelled scallops, halved if large
3 tbsp flour
300 ml/½ pt dry white wine
300 ml/½ pt fish or chicken stock
225 g/8 oz peeled cooked prawns
2 tbsp chopped herbs, such as parsley, tarragon or dill
juice of ½ lemon
salt and freshly ground black pepper

Preheat the oven to 200C/400F/gas 6.

Cook the potatoes in boiling salted water for about 12 minutes until soft. Drain well and return to the pan briefly to dry them. Mash with half the butter and half the cream until smooth. Season with some nutmeg, salt and pepper to taste.

Meanwhile, melt the remaining butter in a large heavy-based saucepan over a moderate heat. Add the spring onions and cook for 4-5 minutes until they are soft, but not browned. Stir in the tomatoes, mushrooms and scallops and cook for 3 minutes.

Sprinkle over the flour and cook for 1 further minute, then remove from the heat and gradually stir in the wine and stock. Heat, stirring, until thickened. Cook for 1 minute.

Stir in the remaining cream, the prawns, herbs and lemon juice. Season with salt and pepper. Transfer to a 1.1 litre/2 pt pie dish and either spoon or pipe the potato mixture on top.

Bake in the oven for 25-30 minutes, until the top is browned and the filling is piping hot.

SEAFOOD LASAGNE

SERVES 6

450 g/1 lb mussels
150 ml/¼ pt dry white wine
2 garlic cloves, thinly sliced
170 g/6 oz peeled cooked prawns
225 g/8 oz shelled scallops, sliced
225 g/8 oz skinless fillets of firm white fish, such as cod or whiting, diced
3 tbsp olive oil
1 onion, sliced
1 small green or red sweet pepper, deseeded and chopped
450 g/1 lb tomatoes, deseeded and chopped
1 tbsp chopped parsley
1 tbsp chopped dill
2 tbsp brandy
8 sheets of fresh or dried lasagne verde
45 g/1½ oz Parmesan cheese, grated
salt and freshly ground black pepper
butter, for greasing
FOR THE BECHAMEL SAUCE
30 g/1 oz butter
4 tbsp flour
700 ml/1¼ pt milk
1 bay leaf
large pinch of freshly grated nutmeg

Scrub the mussels and remove any 'beards'. Discard any open mussels that do not close when tapped.

Put the wine and garlic in a large saucepan and bring to the boil. Add the mussels, cover and cook over a high heat for about 3 minutes, until almost all of the mussel shells have opened. Strain, reserving the cooking liquor. Discard any unopened mussels, reserve a few good-looking open whole mussels for garnish and shell the rest. Set aside with the prawns, scallops and fish.

Heat the oil in a large shallow pan over a moderate heat. Add the onion and sweet pepper and cook them for 4-5 minutes until they have just softened.

Stir in the tomatoes and the reserved mussel cooking liquor. Season with salt and pepper. Bring to the boil. Then lower the heat, cover and simmer for 10 minutes. Stir in the scallops, fish, herbs and brandy and cook for a further 2 minutes. Add the prawns and shelled mussels and remove from the heat.

Preheat the oven to 190C/375F/gas5 and lightly grease a shallow baking dish with butter.

Cook the lasagne in a large pan of rapidly boiling salted water until just tender. Drain well.

Make the bechamel sauce: melt the butter in a small heavy-based saucepan. Add the flour and cook, stirring constantly, for 1-2 minutes. Gradually add the milk, stirring constantly. Still stirring, cook until smooth and thickened.

Add the bay leaf and season with nutmeg, salt and pepper. Cook over a gentle heat for about 5 minutes, then remove the bay leaf.

Fill the prepared dish with alternating layers of seafood mixture, pasta and sauce, finishing with a layer of sauce. Sprinkle with grated Parmesan and bake in the oven for 30-35 minutes, until the top has browned.

Serve hot, garnished with the reserved open mussels still in their shells.

For a more economical version of the SEAFOOD LASAGNE, omit the scallops and use only 115 g/4 oz of prawns. In their place add a layer of 285 g/10 oz mixed chopped vegetables, such as celery, courgettes, broccoli and mushrooms, which have been lightly sautéed in butter.

To be absolutely sure of the cleanliness of MUSSELS and to remove lingering grittiness it is a good idea to soak them in salted water for a couple of hours before further preparation. Adding some oatmeal or flour to the water can make the mussels plumper and tastier.

MUSSELS WITH CREAM AND BACON

SERVES 4–6

1.35 k/3 lb mussels
30 g/1 oz butter
2 tbsp olive oil
1 onion, chopped
2 garlic cloves, finely chopped
85 g/3 oz smoked bacon, chopped
1 bay leaf
2 tbsp coarsely chopped oregano
350 g/12 oz tomatoes, peeled, deseeded and quartered
300 ml/½ pt dry white wine
100 ml/3½ fl oz double cream
salt and freshly ground black pepper
sprigs of flat-leaf parsley, to garnish

Scrub the mussels and remove any 'beards'. Discard any open mussels that do not close when tapped.

Melt the butter with the olive oil in a large saucepan over a moderate heat. Add the onion, garlic and bacon and cook for 5 minutes, until just beginning to colour.

Stir in the bay leaf, oregano, tomatoes and wine. Bring to the boil. Add the mussels to the pan, cover and cook for 4–5 minutes until almost all of the shells open. Using a slotted spoon, transfer the mussels to a plate, discarding any that do not open. Set aside.

Cook the sauce over a high heat, uncovered, for 5 minutes to reduce the liquid by about one-third. Meanwhile remove about half of the mussels from their shells. Discard these shells.

Stir the cream and all the mussels into the sauce and season with salt and pepper.

Garnish with the sprigs of parsley to serve, accompanied by warm crusty bread or pasta.

Left: Mussels with Cream and Bacon; right: Prawn and Scallop Pie (page 28)

MEAT, POULTRY AND GAME

Although beef and veal were the reserve of wealthier land-owners, most country folk kept at least some pigs and chickens, and sheep roamed otherwise uncultivated hillsides. So even those families who could not regularly afford a roast joint for Sunday lunch could manage a hot-pot or stew flavoured with lamb or pork chops, or a chicken pie. Some wild game, especially rabbits and small birds, was also available to all and features strongly in traditional country cooking.

The pig was always the real mainstay of the rural kitchen, however, as every part of it could be put to good use – from its trotters to its crispy skin – and it lent itself so well to being preserved as flavoursome hams and bacon.

Left: Steak and Mushroom Pudding (page 35); right: Beef and Guinness Pie (page 34)

BEEF FILLET IN BACON WITH MUSTARD SAUCE

SERVES 6

30 g/1 oz butter
2 shallots, finely chopped
1 garlic clove, crushed
450 g/1 lb mushrooms, finely chopped
1 tbsp chopped parsley
115 g/4 oz smooth liver pâté
10 slices of rindless back bacon
900 g/2 lb piece of beef fillet, trimmed of fat
1 onion, chopped
2 carrots, chopped
1 celery stalk, chopped
1 tbsp flour
2 tbsp Dijon mustard
150 ml/¼ pt red wine
150 ml/¼ pt beef stock
salt and freshly ground black pepper

Preheat the oven to 200C/400F/gas6.

Melt the butter in a heavy-based saucepan over a moderate heat. Add the shallots and garlic and cook for 3 minutes, until translucent.

Add the mushrooms and season with salt and pepper. Continue cooking, stirring, for a few minutes. Increase the heat and cook rapidly to evaporate the liquid, until the contents of the pan are fairly dry.

Remove from the heat and add the parsley and pâté to the pan. Mix thoroughly and leave to cool.

Lay the bacon slices, overlapping slightly, on a board. Spread the mushroom pâté mixture over the bacon, then place the beef fillet on top. Season with a little more pepper and wrap the bacon up and around the beef, securing it in place with wooden cocktail sticks or string.

Put the chopped onion, carrot and celery in the base of a roasting pan and place the wrapped beef on top. Cook the beef in the oven for 40 minutes for rare, 50 minutes for medium.

Make the sauce: strain the cooking juices into a small saucepan. Add the flour and mix until smooth. Cook over a moderate heat for 2 minutes, stirring. Stir in the mustard followed by the wine and stock. Bring to the boil, stirring, and simmer for 5 minutes.

Season the sauce to taste and serve with the beef.

BEEF AND GUINNESS PIE

2 tbsp flour, plus more for dusting
½ tsp mustard powder
675 g/1½ lb braising steak, cubed
4 tbsp olive oil
12 baby onions, peeled
250 ml/8 fl oz Guinness stout
250 ml/8 fl oz beef stock
sprig of thyme
2 tbsp Worcestershire sauce
450 g/1 lb Quick Puff Pastry (see page 44)
1 egg, beaten
milk, to glaze
salt and freshly ground black pepper

Mix the flour and mustard powder in a large bowl together with some salt and pepper. Add the meat and toss to coat it well in the seasoned flour.

Heat the oil in a flameproof casserole or large heavy-based pan over a high heat. Add the onions and cook for 3-4 minutes to brown them. Using a slotted spoon, remove the onions and set aside.

Add the cubes of meat to the pan, in batches if necessary, and brown them on all sides.

Stir in the Guinness, stock, thyme and the Worcestershire sauce. Bring to the boil then lower the heat, cover and simmer for about 2 hours, until the meat is tender. After 1½ hours, stir in the reserved onions and remove the thyme.

Preheat the oven to 220C/425F/gas7. Transfer the filling to a pie dish, piling the meat in the centre to prevent the pastry from sinking during cooking.

On a floured surface, roll out the pastry to a round big enough to cover the pie generously. Dampen the rim of the pie dish with water and cut a long strip of pastry to fit around it. Once this is firmly in place, dampen its top with a little more water. Use the remaining pastry to cover the pie, trim the edges and crimp to seal.

Make a slit in the centre to allow the steam to escape and brush with a mixture of the beaten egg and some milk to glaze. Use the pastry trimmings to decorate the pie and glaze again.

Bake in the oven for 25-30 minutes, until the pastry is well risen and golden brown.

STEAK AND MUSHROOM PUDDING

4 tbsp oil
675 g/1½ lb braising steak
1 onion, chopped
2 tbsp flour
sprig of thyme
sprig of marjoram
1 tbsp Worcestershire sauce
150 ml/¼ pt beef stock
5 tbsp port
115 g/4 oz small button mushrooms
salt and freshly ground black pepper
FOR THE SUET–CRUST PASTRY
350 g/12 oz self-raising flour
1 tsp salt
170 g/6 oz shredded suet

Heat the oil in a large heavy-based saucepan over a high heat. Brown the meat, in batches if necessary, stirring to colour on all sides. Transfer to a plate.

Add the onion to the pan and cook for 5 minutes over a moderate heat until softened. Stir in the flour and cook for a further minute. Add the herbs and Worcestershire sauce to the pan and gradually stir in the stock and port. Heat until thickened.

Return the meat to the pan and bring to the boil. Season, cover and simmer gently for 45 minutes.

Meanwhile, prepare the suet-crust pastry: sieve the flour and salt into a large mixing bowl and stir in the suet. Gradually stir in 250-300 ml/8-10 fl oz of cold water to form a soft, but not sticky, dough.

Grease a 1.1 litre/2 pt pudding basin. Turn the dough out on a lightly floured surface and knead gently. Roll it out to form a large circle about 6 mm/¼ in thick. Cut a quarter wedge from the dough and set it aside to be used for the lid.

Use the remaining dough to line the prepared pudding basin, pressing the edges to form a seal. Spoon alternate layers of the filling and the mushrooms into the basin.

Re-roll the remaining pastry and use it to cover the pudding. Crimp the edges to seal and trim away any excess pastry. Cover with a pleated piece of greaseproof paper and the same of foil and secure tightly with string.

Put the pudding in a large saucepan which has a tight-fitting lid. Pour in enough hot water to come about three-quarters of the way up the basin, cover and steam the pudding for about 2 hours, topping up the water level occasionally to prevent it boiling dry.

The BEEF AND GUINNESS PIE *may be made with any stout or dark beer. Try adding some canned oysters for a traditional treat.*

LEG OF LAMB WITH WHOLE ROAST GARLIC

SERVES 4–6

1 leg of lamb, weighing about 1.5 k/3½ lb
1 tsp mustard powder
3 large rosemary sprigs
3 whole heads of garlic
1 tbsp olive oil
175 ml/6 fl oz port
4 tbsp redcurrant jelly
1 tsp cornflour
salt and freshly ground black pepper
rosemary sprigs, to garnish (optional)
redcurrant sprigs, to garnish (optional)

Preheat the oven to 230C/450F/gas8. Sprinkle the lamb with salt, pepper and mustard and rub in well.

Cut 2 of the rosemary sprigs into 3.5 cm/1½ in pieces. Using a pointed knife, make incisions deep into the lamb and insert the rosemary pieces into them.

Place the remaining rosemary sprig in a roasting pan and place the lamb on top. Roast in the oven for 20 minutes, then lower the oven temperature to 180C/350F/gas4 and continue cooking for a further 1½ hours. The lamb should still be a little pink inside.

About 40 minutes before the end of the cooking time, brush the heads of garlic with the olive oil and add them to the roasting pan.

Transfer the cooked lamb and garlic to a warmed serving platter and leave to rest for 12–15 minutes before carving the lamb and serving.

Meanwhile, prepare the sauce: pour off any excess fat in the roasting pan. Add the port to the pan together with 100 ml/3½ fl oz of water. Bring to the boil and cook over a moderate to high heat for 2 minutes, stirring and scraping up the sediment with a wooden spoon.

Add the redcurrant jelly and stir until dissolved. Cook for 1 minute. Blend the cornflour with 2 tablespoons of cold water and add to the sauce. Stir until thickened.

Season the sauce to taste and serve with the lamb, garnished with rosemary and redcurrants if using, and the roast garlic.

IRISH HOT-POT

8–12 lamb chops from the middle neck
2 onions, thinly sliced
225 g/8 oz carrot, thickly sliced
675 g/1½ lb potatoes, thinly sliced
1 tbsp rosemary spikes (optional)
300 ml/½ pt well-flavoured beef or lamb stock
30 g/1 oz butter
salt and freshly ground black pepper
chopped parsley, to garnish

Preheat the oven to 160C/325F/gas3.

Trim any excess fat from the chops and layer them in a large casserole dish with the onions, carrots, potatoes and rosemary, if using. Season each layer with salt and pepper and finish with a layer of overlapping slices of potato.

Bring the stock to the boil and pour it over the casserole. Dot the butter over the surface. Cover tightly with a lid or foil and bake in the oven for 2 hours.

Remove the lid from the casserole and increase the oven temperature to 220C/425F/gas7 for 15–20 minutes, until the potatoes are browned.

Serve the hot-pot in soup plates, sprinkled with chopped parsley.

Left: Leg of Lamb with Whole Roast Garlic; right: Gratin Dauphinois (page 48)

BEEF AND LAMB WITH ALMONDS

3 tbsp olive oil
45 g/1½ oz blanched almonds
350 g/12 oz stewing beef, cubed
350 g/12 oz lamb, cubed
1 onion, chopped
2 garlic cloves, chopped
2 tsp coriander seeds, lightly crushed
¼ tsp ground allspice
300 ml/½ pt beef stock
115 g/4 oz no-soak dried apricots, halved
salt and freshly ground black pepper
chopped coriander, to garnish

Preheat the oven to 180C/350F/gas4.

Heat 1 tablespoon of the olive oil in a large heavy-based saucepan over a moderate heat. Add the almonds and cook, stirring, for 2-3 minutes until golden brown. Transfer to a plate and set aside.

Add the remaining oil to the pan, increase the heat slightly and cook the meat, in batches if necessary, until browned on all sides. Using a slotted spoon, transfer the meat to a large ovenproof casserole.

Add the onion, garlic and spices to the pan and cook over a moderate heat for 5 minutes, stirring frequently. Pour in the stock and bring to the boil. Add the contents of the pan to the casserole. Season with salt and pepper. Cover and cook in the oven for 1 hour.

At the end of this time, add the apricots and browned almonds to the casserole and mix well. Cover again and return the casserole to the oven for a further 45-60 minutes, until the meat is tender.

Adjust the seasoning, if necessary. Serve sprinkled with chopped fresh coriander and accompanied by basmati rice.

NAVARIN OF LAMB

4 tbsp olive oil
675 g/1½ lb lamb fillet from the shoulder, diced
12 baby onions
8-12 baby carrots
6 small baby turnips
2 garlic cloves, chopped
1 tbsp flour
575 ml/1 pt well-flavoured stock
300 ml/½ pt red wine
bouquet garni
8 small new potatoes
salt and freshly ground black pepper
chopped parsley, to garnish
FOR THE CROUTONS
4 large slices of white bread, crusts removed
3 tbsp light olive oil

Heat 2 tablespoons of the oil in a large heavy-based saucepan over a high heat. Add the meat and cook, stirring, until the pieces are browned on all sides. Using a slotted spoon, transfer the meat to a plate.

Put the remaining oil in the pan. Add the onions, carrots and turnips and cook for 5 minutes, stirring, over a medium to high heat. Using a slotted spoon, transfer the vegetables to a plate and reserve.

Add the garlic to the pan and cook for 1 minute. Stir in the flour and cook, stirring, for 2 minutes. Then gradually stir in the stock and wine. Bring to the boil, then return the meat to the pan. Add the bouquet garni and season with salt and pepper. Bring back to the boil. Then lower the heat, cover and simmer for 45 minutes, stirring occasionally.

Add the reserved vegetables and the potatoes to the pan. Cover and continue to simmer for 30 minutes. Then remove the lid and cook uncovered for a further 10-15 minutes to allow the sauce to reduce slightly.

While the sauce is reducing, make the croutons:

NAVARIN OF LAMB *is a traditional French lamb stew and derives its name from* navet, *the French term for the turnip. When made this way with spring vegetables, the dish is also known as 'Navarin printanier'.*

cut the slices of bread into triangles or use a pastry cutter to cut out circles or other shapes. Heat the oil in a frying pan over a moderate to high heat. When the oil is really hot, add the bread, a few pieces at a time, and cook for a few seconds on each side until golden and crisp. Drain on paper towels.

Adjust the seasoning of the navarin, sprinkle with parsley and serve with the croutons.

PORK WITH JUNIPER, CELERY AND PRUNES

3 tbsp oil
675 g/1½ lb pork tenderloin, cut into 3.5 cm/1½ in pieces
2 shallots, finely chopped
2 celery stalks, cut into matchstick strips
2 tsp juniper berries, lightly crushed
250 ml/9 fl oz dry white wine
3 tbsp sherry
1 bay leaf
4 fresh sage leaves, shredded
12 no-soak prunes
salt and freshly ground black pepper
fresh sage leaves, to garnish

Heat the oil in a large saucepan over a high heat. Add the pork and brown on all sides. Using a slotted spoon, transfer to a plate and set aside.

Add the shallots to the pan and cook over a moderate heat for 4-5 minutes to soften. Add the celery and juniper and cook for 2 minutes.

Add the wine, sherry and herbs and bring to the boil. Return the meat to the pan, cover and simmer for 20 minutes.

Add the prunes and continue cooking, uncovered, for 10 minutes until the sauce is reduced by about half and the pork is tender. Adjust the seasoning, if necessary and serve immediately garnished with fresh sage leaves.

NORMANDY PORK CHOPS

3 tbsp oil
4 pork or veal chops, about 2.5 cm/1 in thick
4 tbsp brandy, preferably Calvados
FOR THE SAUCE
300 ml/½ pt double cream
30 g/1 oz butter
1 tbsp chopped parsley
salt and freshly ground black pepper
FOR THE GLAZED APPLES
2 dessert apples
1 tbsp lemon juice
30 g/1 oz butter
large pinch of sugar

Heat the oil in a large heavy-based frying pan over a high heat. Add the chops and brown them on both sides. Add the brandy to the pan and carefully set it aflame. Allow the flames to subside and season with salt and pepper.

Lower the heat and cook the chops for about 3-4 minutes each side, until done. Transfer the chops to a warmed serving plate and keep warm.

Make the sauce: add the cream and butter to the pan, stirring well to scrape up all the sediment. Stir in the parsley and cook for 3-4 minutes, until the sauce begins to thicken. Season and keep warm.

Make the glazed apples: peel, core and cut the apples into thick wedges and toss these in the lemon juice. Melt the butter in a frying pan over a moderate heat and add the apples. Sprinkle with the sugar and fry for 2-3 minutes to brown.

Serve the chops accompanied by the glazed apples and the sauce.

The region of NORMANDY produces most of France's apple crop and for this reason it is a centre of the manufacture of cider and Calvados, the cider brandy. It is also the province most associated with dairy products. Hence dishes with apples, cider, Calvados or lashings of butter and cream characterize the cooking of Normandy.

CASSOULET

SERVES 6

2 onions
2 cloves
450 g/1 lb dried haricot beans, soaked
overnight in cold water
6 tbsp olive oil
2 garlic cloves, crushed
350 g/12 oz tomatoes, peeled and coarsely chopped
1 tbsp tomato paste
bouquet garni
6 lamb cutlets
350 g/12 oz Toulouse sausages, cut into 5 cm/2 in pieces
350 g/12 oz belly of pork, diced
5 tbsp fresh white breadcrumbs
salt and freshly ground black pepper

Chop one of the onions and stick the cloves into the other. Drain the beans and place them in a saucepan. Add the clove-studded onion to the beans together with enough water just to cover. Bring to the boil and boil for 10 minutes. Drain well, reserving the onion, and set aside.

Heat 3 tablespoons of the olive oil in a large heavy-based saucepan over a moderate heat. Add the chopped onion and the garlic and cook for 4–5 minutes until soft. Stir in the drained beans, the tomatoes, tomato paste and bouquet garni and cook for 3 minutes.

Add 1.1 litre/2 pt of water to the pan and bring to the boil. Lower the heat, cover and cook over a gentle heat for 40 minutes.

Towards the end of that time, preheat the oven to 180C/350F/gas 4. In a large frying pan, heat the remaining oil and brown the lamb cutlets and Toulouse sausages, in batches if necessary. Remove

Top: Cassoulet; bottom: Normandy Pork Chops (page 39)

and drain on paper towels. Repeat with the belly of pork.

Remove the clove-studded onion from the cooked beans. Season the beans with salt and pepper and transfer half to a large ovenproof dish or casserole. Arrange the cooked meats on top and cover with the remaining beans.

Cover and bake in the oven for about 1 hour. Then remove the lid and sprinkle with the breadcrumbs. Return to the oven, uncovered, for a further 30–45 minutes.

SAUTÉED KIDNEYS WITH ONIONS AND SOUR CREAM

SERVES 4–6 AS A STARTER
OR 3 AS A MAIN COURSE

2 tbsp light olive oil
1 small onion, chopped
1 garlic clove, crushed
45 g/1½ oz butter
12 lambs' kidneys, halved and cored
2 tbsp brandy
100 ml/3½ fl oz sour cream
2 tbsp snipped chives, parsley, tarragon or coriander
salt and freshly ground black pepper

Heat the oil in a large heavy-based frying pan over a moderate heat. Add the onion and garlic and cook for 4 minutes to soften.

Add half of the butter and the kidneys. Cook, stirring, for about 2 minutes to brown the kidneys.

Stir in the brandy and allow to simmer for 4–5 minutes. Add the remaining butter, sour cream and half the herbs to the pan. Heat gently, stirring. Season with salt and pepper.

Garnish with the remaining herbs and serve with melba toast as a starter or as a main course accompanied by rice and a green vegetable.

CASSOULET *is the traditional bean stew of south-west France. Flavoured with garlic, herbs and pork, it may contain a wide variety of added meats, such as the lamb and sausages used here, or even preserved duck or goose portions. If* TOULOUSE SAUSAGES *are unavailable, use Cumberland or any other good pure pork sausages.*

RAISED POULTRY PIE

SERVES 6

FOR THE FILLING
*675 g/1½ lb boneless chicken or turkey meat, cut
into thin strips*
225 g/8 oz chicken or turkey livers, chopped
225 g/8 oz streaky bacon, chopped
1 tbsp green peppercorns in brine, drained
2 garlic cloves, chopped
3 tbsp sherry
salt and freshly ground black pepper
FOR THE HOT WATER CRUST PASTRY
140 g/5 oz lard, diced, plus more for greasing
450 g/1 lb flour
1 tsp salt
1 egg, beaten
milk, to glaze

First make the filling: mix all the ingredients well in a large bowl and set aside.

Preheat the oven to 200C/400F/gas6. Grease a raised pie mould or 15 cm/6 in loose-bottomed cake tin with some lard.

Make the pastry: sieve the flour and salt into a large bowl. In a small saucepan, heat the lard and 125 ml/4 fl oz of water until melted. Bring to the boil then pour over the flour. Mix thoroughly to a soft dough.

Turn out on a lightly floured surface and knead until just smooth. While still warm, roll out three-quarters and use to line the prepared mould or tin.

Fill the pie with the prepared mixture and roll out the remaining pastry to make a lid. Crimp the edges of the pastry to seal and make a few steam holes in the lid. Use pastry trimmings to decorate the top of the pie. Mix the beaten egg and some milk and brush the top with this glaze.

Bake for 30 minutes, then lower the temperature to 180C/350F/gas4 and cook for another 1¼ hours. Allow to cool in the tin and serve cold.

CHICKEN WITH GARLIC AND OLIVES

*8 small chicken portions (preferably legs and
thighs), skinned*
sprig of thyme
sprig of rosemary
1 bay leaf
3 tbsp olive oil
1 large onion, thinly sliced
5 garlic cloves, halved
200 ml/7 fl oz dry white wine
12 stoned black olives
12 stoned green olives, sliced
salt and freshly ground black pepper

Rinse the chicken pieces, pat them dry and season. Tie the herbs into a bundle with string.

Heat the oil in a large heavy-based saucepan over a moderate to high heat. Add the chicken portions and brown them on all sides.

Add the herbs, onion and garlic and cook for a further 5 minutes. Stir in the wine and bring to the boil. Then lower the heat, cover and cook for 30 minutes.

Using a slotted spoon, transfer the chicken to a warmed serving platter. Stir the juices in the pan thoroughly to blend the garlic.

Add the olives to the pan and cook, uncovered, for about 5 minutes to reduce the sauce by about one-third. Discard the herbs, adjust the seasoning to taste and pour the sauce over the chicken pieces.

Serve sprinkled with chopped fresh parsley to garnish.

Left: Raised Poultry Pie; right: Celeriac and Swede Purée and Carrot and Parsnip Purée from the Trio of Vegetable Purées (page 48)

ROAST DUCK WITH BABY TURNIPS

1 oven-ready duckling, weighing about 1.8 k/4 lb
45 g/1½ oz butter
675 g/1½ lb small baby turnips
2-3 tsp soft light brown sugar
salt and freshly ground black pepper
sprigs of herbs, to garnish
FOR THE SAUCE
2 shallots, finely chopped
1 tsp grated zest from an unwaxed lemon
150 ml/¼ pt dry white wine
150 ml/¼ pt chicken stock
5 tbsp Marsala
2 tsp cornflour

Preheat the oven to 200C/400F/gas6.

Using a needle or skewer, prick the skin of the duck all over to let the fat run. Season the duck well with salt and pepper, rubbing it well into the skin. Place the bird on a rack in a roasting pan and cover loosely with foil.

Roast for 1-1¼ hours, removing the foil halfway through cooking to allow the skin to brown and crisp. As the foil is removed, take 3 tablespoons of duck fat from the roasting pan and reserve.

Make the sauce: heat the reserved duck fat in a small heavy-based saucepan over a low heat. Add the shallots and cook gently for 5-7 minutes, until soft and just beginning to brown.

Stir in the lemon zest, wine and stock. Bring to the boil, cover and simmer for 10 minutes. Stir in the Marsala. Blend the cornflour with 2 tablespoons of cold water, add this to the sauce and stir until thickened. Season to taste, then cover and set aside.

Melt the butter in a large heavy-based pan. Add the turnips and cook, stirring, over a medium heat for 2 minutes. Add 150 ml/¼ pt of water to the pan together with the sugar, salt and pepper. Bring to the

If BABY TURNIPS are unavailable, glaze some baby onions in the same way and serve the duck garnished with these and some fresh green peas.

boil. Cook, uncovered and stirring frequently, for about 15 minutes until the turnips are just tender and the liquid has evaporated to a caramelized glaze.

Serve the duck on a warmed platter, surrounded by the glazed baby turnips and garnished with sprigs of herbs. Gently reheat the sauce to accompany it.

GAME PIE

SERVES 6

2-4 game birds, depending on size (about 1.35 k/3 lb)
6 black peppercorns
bouquet garni
2 onions
55 g/2 oz butter
225 g/8 oz small-cap mushrooms, thickly sliced
115 g/4 oz streaky bacon, chopped
1 tbsp flour
3 hard-boiled eggs, shelled and quartered
1 tbsp chopped parsley
salt and freshly ground black pepper
FOR THE QUICK PUFF PASTRY
(makes about 450 g/1 lb)
225 g/8 oz strong white flour
170 g/6 oz chilled butter, cut into small dice
1 tsp lemon juice
about 150 ml/¼ pt iced water
1 egg, beaten
milk, to glaze

Make the pastry: sieve the flour with a pinch of salt into a mixing bowl. Stir in the butter, add the lemon juice and mix in sufficient iced water to form a firm dough. Do not break up the butter pieces. Turn the dough out on a floured surface and form into a brick shape. Wrap in film and chill for 10 minutes.

On a well-floured surface, lightly roll out the pastry to a long rectangle about 6 mm/¼ in thick. It should be about three times longer than it is wide.

Fold the bottom third up and the top third down. Press the edges lightly with the rolling pin. Cover with film and chill again for 10 minutes.

Return the pastry to the floured surface, but giving it a quarter turn clockwise. Roll out to a rectangle again and fold and chill as before. Repeat this turning, rolling and chilling process twice more. Wrap in film and chill for at least 30 minutes.

While the pastry is chilling put the birds, peppercorns and bouquet garni in a large pan. Quarter one of the onions and slice the other. Add the quartered onion to the pan. Add just enough water to cover and bring to the boil. Lower the heat, cover and simmer for 45-60 minutes, until the meat is easily separated from the bone. Transfer the birds to a plate and allow to cool. Strain the stock.

Preheat the oven to 220C/425F/gas7.

When the birds are cool enough to handle, pull the meat from the carcasses, keeping it in fairly large pieces. Arrange these in the bottom of a pie dish.

Melt the butter in a heavy-based saucepan over a moderate heat. Add the sliced onion, the mushrooms and bacon and cook, stirring, for 5 minutes. Stir in the flour and cook for a further minute. Gradually stir in 300 ml/½ pt of the reserved stock and bring to the boil. Simmer gently for 5 minutes to give a rich sauce.

Add the egg quarters to the pie dish, piling them slightly in the centre. Sprinkle with the parsley and season with salt and pepper. Cover with the sauce.

Roll out the pastry to a round large enough to cover the pie dish generously. Dampen the rim of the pie dish with water and cut a long strip of pastry to fit around it. Once in place, dampen this and use the remaining pastry to cover the pie. Crimp the edges.

Brush the pastry with egg and milk mixture to glaze. Lightly mark a lattice pattern in the pastry.

Bake in the oven for about 30 minutes, until the pastry is well risen and golden brown. Serve hot.

Roast Duck with Baby Turnips

VEGETABLES AND PULSES

The wisely economical ways of country folk were reflected in the manner in which they cooked their vegetables. Tasty tender spring vegetables were given the lightest of cooking and served very plainly. In autumn and winter, however, older tougher vegetables were quite commonly baked in the oven with the bread or other dishes, like the *Gratin Dauphinois*, or stewed over an open hearth. Some such stews of vegetables or beans were even cleverly enhanced to make meals in themselves, as in the *Bean Stew with Herb Dumplings* or the *Pumpkin Stew with Haricots or Barley*. The rich full flavours of some traditional baked vegetable dishes, like *Stuffed Marrow* or *Red Cabbage with Cloves and Chestnuts*, really evoke the spirit of country cooking.

Top: Bean Stew with Herb Dumplings (page 49); bottom: Vegetable Gratin (page 48)

One of the classics of French cuisine, GRATIN DAUPHINOIS turns ordinary potatoes into a luxurious treat and may also be enriched by the addition of one or two eggs.

GRATIN DAUPHINOIS

SERVES 4–6

30 g/1 oz butter
900 g/2 lb potatoes, peeled and very thinly sliced
1 garlic clove, chopped
large pinch of freshly grated nutmeg
300 ml/½ pt double cream
55 g/2 oz Gruyère cheese, grated
salt and freshly ground black pepper

Preheat the oven to 190C/375F/gas5. Use half of the butter to grease a shallow 1.1 litre/2 pt ovenproof dish.

Layer the potatoes in the dish, dotting the layers with the remaining butter and the garlic and seasoning with nutmeg, salt and pepper.

Pour the cream over and bake in the oven for 1¼ hours. Sprinkle with the cheese and return to the oven for 15-20 minutes. Serve hot.

VEGETABLE GRATIN

1 small cauliflower, broken into florets
225 g/8 oz broccoli, broken into florets
white parts only of 4 spring onions, halved
30 g/1 oz butter
30 g/1 oz flour
1 tsp Dijon mustard
450 ml/¾ pt milk
115 g/4 oz mature Cheddar cheese, grated
55 g/2 oz Gruyère cheese, grated
30 g/1 oz hazelnuts, roughly chopped
salt and freshly ground black pepper

Cook the cauliflower, broccoli and spring onions in boiling salted water for 4 minutes. Drain thoroughly and arrange the vegetables in a heatproof serving dish. Keep warm.

Melt the butter in a small heavy-based saucepan, stir in the flour and cook, stirring, for 1-2 minutes. Stir in the mustard and milk and bring to the boil, stirring constantly, until thickened and smooth. Stir in the Cheddar and season with salt and pepper.

Preheat a medium grill. Pour the sauce over the vegetables and sprinkle with the Gruyère and hazelnuts. Cook under the grill until golden brown. Serve hot.

TRIO OF VEGETABLE PURÉES

SERVES 6

FOR THE JERUSALEM ARTICHOKE PURÉE
285 g/10 oz Jerusalem artichokes, diced
170 g/6 oz potato, diced
knob of butter
2 tbsp single cream
large pinch of freshly grated nutmeg
FOR THE CARROT AND PARSNIP PURÉE
170 g/6 oz carrot, sliced
170 g/6 oz parsnip, sliced
knob of butter
½ garlic clove, crushed
FOR THE CELERIAC AND SWEDE PURÉE
225 g/8 oz celeriac
115 g/4 oz swede
knob of butter
squeeze of lemon juice
1 tbsp chopped parsley
salt and freshly ground black pepper

In 3 separate saucepans, cook the vegetables for each purée in boiling water for 8-10 minutes, until soft. Drain the three vegetable mixtures and return them to their saucepans.

Add a knob of butter to each and season with their respective flavourings, salt and pepper. Using a potato masher, mash each until smooth. Serve hot.

RED CABBAGE WITH CLOVES AND CHESTNUTS

SERVES 6

675 g/1½ lb red cabbage, finely shredded
2 small sharp apples, peeled, cored and sliced
2 tsp juniper berries, crushed
1 tbsp fresh rosemary spikes
30 g/1 oz butter
1 tbsp olive oil
1 onion, finely chopped
½ tsp ground cinnamon
4 cloves
2 tbsp redcurrant jelly
2 tbsp red wine vinegar
150 ml/¼ pt port
225 g/8 oz cooked whole chestnuts
salt and freshly ground black pepper
chopped fresh parsley, to garnish

Preheat the oven to 150C/300F/gas2.

Arrange the cabbage and apple in layers in a large casserole dish, seasoning each layer with juniper, rosemary, salt and pepper.

Melt the butter with the oil in a heavy-based saucepan over a moderate heat. Add the onion and cook for 4–5 minutes. Stir in the cinnamon, cloves, redcurrant jelly, vinegar and port. Bring to the boil, stirring until the jelly has dissolved.

Pour this over the cabbage and cover the casserole tightly with foil and a lid. Bake in the oven for 2 hours. Check from time to time to see if all the liquid has evaporated, adding a little more port or water as necessary.

Add the chestnuts to the casserole, cover and return to the oven for 15–20 minutes to warm them through. Serve sprinkled with chopped parsley.

BEAN STEW WITH HERB DUMPLINGS

3 tbsp olive oil
1 onion, chopped
1-2 garlic cloves, crushed
2 celery stalks, chopped
2 carrots, sliced
140 g/5 oz cannellini or black-eye beans, soaked overnight in cold water
bouquet garni
450 g/1 lb tomatoes, peeled and chopped
850 ml/1½ pt well-flavoured chicken or vegetable stock
salt and freshly ground black pepper
FOR THE HERB DUMPLINGS
55 g/2 oz shredded suet
55 g/2 oz fresh white breadcrumbs
55 g/2 oz self-raising flour
3 tbsp chopped mixed herbs

Heat the oil in a large pan over a moderate heat. Add the onion and garlic and sauté for 4 minutes. Stir in the celery and carrots and cook for 2 more minutes.

Add the remaining ingredients and bring to the boil. Season. Lower the heat, cover and simmer for 45 minutes, stirring occasionally.

Towards the end of this time make the dumplings: mix all the ingredients together with about 5 tablespoons of cold water and seasonings to give a firm dough. Shape into 12 balls.

Arrange the dumplings on top of the stew. Cover and continue simmering for 20 minutes, until the dumplings are light and fluffy. Serve at once.

Garnish the BEAN STEW WITH HERB DUMPLINGS *with more chopped herbs for an even more appealing dish.*

HERB AND WILD MUSHROOM RISOTTO

30 g/1 oz dried ceps (porcini)
115 g/4 oz fresh mushrooms, preferably wild
115 g/4 oz butter
1 small onion, finely chopped
350 g/12 oz risotto rice, preferably arborio
150 ml/¼ pt dry white wine
1.1 litre/2 pt hot chicken stock
2 tbsp chopped parsley
2 tbsp chopped sage
3 tbsp freshly grated Parmesan cheese
salt and freshly ground black pepper

Put the dried ceps in a small bowl and cover with warm water. Leave to soak for 20 minutes, then rinse thoroughly, drain and chop, reserving a few for garnish. Halve, slice or quarter the fresh mushrooms according to their size.

Melt half of the butter in a heavy-based saucepan over a moderate heat. Add the onion and cook for 5 minutes to soften.

Stir in the rice and the fresh mushrooms and cook for 2-3 minutes until the rice is translucent. Add the wine and chopped ceps and cook for 3 minutes until all the liquid is absorbed.

Add 575 ml/1 pt of the stock to the pan, lower the heat, cover and simmer for 10 minutes, until the stock is absorbed. Add a further 300 ml/½ pt of stock and continue cooking as before.

Keep checking and adding stock until the rice is tender. Total cooking time will be 20-30 minutes.

Stir in the chopped herbs with the remaining butter, seasonings and half the Parmesan, grated.

Serve, garnished with the reserved ceps and the remaining Parmesan thinly shaved.

Centre: Herb and Wild Mushroom Risotto; right: Spiced Winter Vegetable Casserole (page 52)

PUMPKIN STEW WITH HARICOTS OR BARLEY

SERVES 4–6

170 g/6 oz haricot beans or pearl barley, soaked overnight
in cold water
30 g/1 oz butter
2 tbsp olive oil
1 onion, cut into wedges
1 garlic clove, crushed
350 g/12 oz pumpkin, peeled and diced
2 carrots, sliced
1 small fennel bulb, sliced
1 tsp ground turmeric
1 tsp ground coriander seeds
½ tsp ground cinnamon
4 tomatoes, peeled and quartered
1 tbsp chopped mint
1 tbsp chopped coriander leaves
170 g/6 oz French beans
115 g/4 oz small button mushrooms
850 ml/1½ pt vegetable stock
salt and freshly ground black pepper
garlic bread, to serve

Drain the haricot beans or barley and put them in a saucepan. Cover with water and bring to the boil. Cook for 25 minutes for haricot beans or 15 minutes for barley. Drain and set aside.

Melt the butter with the oil in a large heavy-based saucepan over a moderate heat. Add the onion and garlic and cook for 3 minutes. Stir in the pumpkin, carrots, fennel and spices and continue cooking for 10 minutes, stirring frequently.

Add the beans or barley and all the remaining ingredients to the pan. Season with salt and pepper. Bring to the boil, cover and simmer for 20-25 minutes.

Serve hot with garlic bread.

RISOTTOS *of all types are found in Italian cuisine, from those simply flavoured with cheese or herbs to those containing rich assortments of fish, shellfish, meat or poultry. It is important to use a good stock and the right type of rice, such as arborio, which absorbs a great deal of liquid and gives the desired sticky texture.*

SPICED WINTER VEGETABLE CASSEROLE

SERVES 6

30 g/1 oz butter
1 onion, chopped
10 garlic cloves
225 g/8 oz small turnips, halved
225 g/8 oz kohlrabi, cut into 2.5 cm/1 in cubes
225 g/8 oz carrots, cut into batons
115 g/4 oz Jerusalem artichokes, diced
½ cinnamon stick
4 cloves
large sprig of thyme
300 ml/½ pt red wine
150 ml/¼ pt well-flavoured vegetable stock
2 tsp cornflour
salt and freshly ground black pepper

Preheat the oven to 200C/400F/gas6.

Melt the butter in a large heavy-based saucepan over a moderate heat. Add the onion and garlic cloves and cook, stirring, for 5 minutes, until they begin to brown – but do not let them burn.

Stir in all the vegetables and continue cooking for 3 minutes. Transfer to an ovenproof casserole and add the spices and thyme. Pour over the wine and stock and season. Cover and bake for about 1¼ hours, or until all the vegetables are tender.

Blend the cornflour with 2 tablespoons of cold water and stir this into the stew. Return to the oven, uncovered, for 10 minutes to allow the juices to thicken. Remove the cinnamon and adjust the seasoning to serve.

STUFFED MARROW

SERVES 6

5 tbsp olive oil
2 garlic cloves, chopped
1 shallot, finely chopped
2 sprigs of sage or oregano
675 g/1½ lb fresh broad beans, shelled
350 g/12 oz ripe tomatoes, peeled and chopped
2 tbsp chopped parsley
1 marrow, weighing 1-1.35 k/2¼-3 lb
salt and freshly ground black pepper
4 tbsp freshly grated Parmesan cheese, to serve

Preheat the oven to 190C/375F/gas5.

First prepare the filling: heat 3 tablespoons of the oil in a heavy-based saucepan over a moderate heat. Add the garlic, shallot and herb sprigs and cook for 5 minutes, stirring frequently.

Stir in the beans and tomatoes and season with salt and pepper. Cover and cook for 15 minutes, stirring frequently. Remove the herb sprigs and stir in the chopped parsley.

While the filling is cooking, slice the marrow into six discs. Scoop out the seeds in the centre of each disc together with a little of the inner flesh and arrange the rings that remain in an oiled baking dish.

Brush the marrow flesh with the remaining olive oil. Divide the prepared filling between the marrow rings, cover with foil and bake in the oven for 35 minutes, or until the marrow is tender.

Serve hot, sprinkled with the freshly grated Parmesan cheese.

Top: Red Cabbage with Cloves and Chestnuts (page 49);
bottom: Stuffed Marrow

PUDDINGS AND PIES

*A*bove all, most country cooks prided themselves on their abilities as pie and pudding makers. The abundant supply of local fruit and berries was put to memorable use in a wonderful array of deep pies, tarts, pastries and puddings. Seasonal gluts of fruit which could not be used immediately were made into compotes, jams and jellies or bottled in syrup or alcohol. These preserves would, in turn, be baked into pies and puddings in the winter months. Toppings used ranged from simple sweet shortcrust and puff pastry to easy scone dough for cobblers and the even more simple crumbles. To people the world over the idea of traditional country cooking means the simple glories of apple pies, fruit crumbles or steamed treacle pudding.

Clockwise from the left: Pear Frangipane Tart (page 57), Crème Brûlée (page 56) and Creamed Rice Pudding (page 56)

The SPICED FRUIT COMPOTE WITH MASCARPONE *makes a simple but elegant dessert. Replace the wine with apple, orange or pear juice, however, and it becomes a refreshing breakfast treat. Italian Mascarpone cheese is now widely available.*

CRÈME BRÛLÉE *or 'burnt cream' is more traditionally caramelized with a salamander heated in an open fire.*

CREAMED RICE PUDDING

30 g/1 oz butter
55 g/2 oz pudding rice
30 g/1 oz caster sugar
strip of rind from an unwaxed lemon
300 ml/½ pt milk
300 ml/½ pt single cream
large pinch of freshly grated nutmeg
fresh fruit, fruit compote or pouring cream, to serve

Preheat the oven to 160C/325F/gas3. Use a little of the butter to grease an 850 ml/1½ pt baking dish.

In a sieve or colander, rinse the rice under running water, then put it into the prepared dish with the sugar, lemon rind, milk and cream. Stir until the sugar is dissolved.

Bake for 1 hour, stirring twice. Dot the remaining butter over the surface and sprinkle with nutmeg.

Return to the oven and continue baking for about 45 minutes, until the rice is soft and the top is browned. Serve hot or cold, with fruit or cream.

SPICED FRUIT COMPOTE WITH MASCARPONE

450 g/1 lb mixed dried fruit, such as apricots, prunes, apple rings, pears and figs
30 g/1 oz soft light brown sugar
300 ml/½ pt sweet dessert wine
3 whole cloves
1 cinnamon stick
170 g/6 oz Mascarpone cheese
grated zest of 2 unwaxed lemons

Put the all the ingredients except the cheese and half the lemon zest in a pan with 300 ml/½ pt of water.

Bring to the boil then lower the heat, cover and simmer for 45-50 minutes, until the fruit is plump and the liquid is syrupy. Discard the cinnamon.

Serve the compote either warm or chilled, with the Mascarpone spooned over it and a little of the reserved lemon zest sprinkled over the top.

CRÈME BRÛLÉE

SERVES 6

575 ml/1 pt double cream
1 vanilla pod
4 egg yolks
2 tbsp caster sugar
4 tbsp demerara sugar
fresh fruits in season, such as summer berries or exotic fruits, to serve

Put the cream and vanilla pod in a small saucepan. Heat gently until almost boiling. Remove from the heat, cover and leave to infuse for 30 minutes.

Preheat the oven to 130C/275F/gas1.

Place the egg yolks in a mixing bowl, add the caster sugar and beat well to mix. Reheat the cream until almost boiling. Pour this over the egg yolks, beating with a wire whisk at the same time.

Place the bowl over a pan of simmering water and whisk lightly until the mixture thickens to coat the back of a spoon. Divide the mixture between six 125 ml/4 fl oz ramekins.

Arrange the ramekins in a deep roasting pan and pour in warm water to a depth of 2.5 cm/1 in. Bake in the oven for 30-35 minutes.

Remove the ramekins from the water bath and allow to cool. Chill for at least 1 hour, or up to 24.

Preheat a hot grill. Sprinkle the demerara sugar over the tops of the ramekins. Grill for 3-4 minutes to caramelize the tops.

Allow to cool and then chill for at least 2 hours before serving, accompanied by fresh fruits.

PEAR FRANGIPANE TART

SERVES 6

85 g/3 oz butter, plus more for greasing
85 g/3 oz vanilla sugar
1 egg plus 1 extra yolk, beaten
30 g/1 oz flour
few drops of almond essence
85 g/3 oz ground almonds
3 small ripe dessert pears
2 tsp lemon juice
crème fraîche or cream, to serve
FOR THE RICH SUGAR PASTRY
(makes about 450 g/1 lb)
225 g/8 oz flour
pinch of salt
115 g/4 oz butter, cubed
55 g/2 oz caster sugar
2 egg yolks
2 tbsp iced water
1 tsp lemon juice

Preheat the oven to 200C/400F/gas6 and grease a deep 23 cm/9 in flan ring or loose-bottomed flan tin with butter.

Make the pastry: sieve the flour and salt into a bowl. Lightly rub in the butter until the mixture resembles breadcrumbs, then stir in the sugar.

Mix together the egg yolks, iced water and lemon juice. Using a palette knife, mix this into the flour to form a firm dough.

Turn the dough out on a floured surface and knead lightly. Wrap in film and chill for 20 minutes.

Use the pastry to line the prepared flan ring or tin. Prick the base and fill with baking beans. Bake blind in the oven for 10 minutes.

Remove the baking beans and return to the oven for a further 5 minutes to cook the base. Reduce the oven temperature to 180C/350F/gas4.

Make the frangipane cream filling: beat together

the butter and vanilla sugar until light and fluffy. Beat in the egg and egg yolk and then stir in the flour, almond essence and ground almonds. Spread two-thirds of this filling over the base of the prepared flan case.

Peel, core and halve the pears then slice them thinly across the width. Arrange the slices in the flan case and brush with lemon juice.

Spoon the remaining frangipane cream around the pears and bake the tart in the oven for 30-35 minutes, until the filling is firm and golden brown.

Serve warm with crème fraîche or cream.

BAKED SULTANA AND LEMON CHEESECAKE

SERVES 8

55 g/2 oz butter, plus more for greasing
225 g/8 oz digestive biscuits, crushed
icing sugar, for dusting
FOR THE FILLING
550 g/1¼ lb cream cheese
85 g/3 oz caster sugar
55 g/2 oz ground almonds
juice and grated zest of 2 unwaxed lemons
85 g/3 oz sultanas
3 eggs, beaten

Preheat the oven to 180C/350F/gas4. Grease the base of a deep 20 cm/8 in loose-bottomed cake tin with some butter and line it with greaseproof paper.

Melt the butter in a pan and stir in the biscuits. Mix well and use to line the base of the prepared tin, pressing down well with the back of a spoon.

Make the filling: mix all the ingredients and pour into the tin. Bake for 40-45 minutes, until just set.

Allow to cool in the tin, then chill for at least 1 hour. Transfer to a serving plate and dredge with icing sugar to serve.

The term FRANGIPANE *was first used of almond-flavoured pastry cream in eighteenth-century Paris.*

KEY LIME PIE

SERVES 6–8

55 g/2 oz butter, plus more for greasing
450 g/1 lb Rich Sugar Pastry (see page 57)
4 tbsp cornflour
juice and grated zest of 4 unwaxed limes
115 g/4 oz caster sugar
3 egg yolks
FOR THE MERINGUE TOPPING
3 egg whites
pinch of salt
170 g/6 oz caster sugar

KEY LIME PIE *is so named after America's Florida Keys, the part of the world from which it originated.*

Preheat the oven to 200C/400F/gas6 and grease a deep 23 cm/9 in loose-bottomed flan tin with butter.

Roll out the pastry and use to line the prepared flan tin. Prick the base with a fork and fill with baking beans. Bake blind in the oven for 10 minutes, then remove the baking beans and return to the oven for a further 5 minutes to cook the base. Reduce the oven temperature to 180C/350F/gas4.

In a small bowl, mix the cornflour to a paste with a little of a measured 300 ml/½ pt of water. Put the rest of the water in a saucepan with the lime juice and sugar. Bring to the boil. Pour in the cornflour mixture, stirring constantly, and cook for 2-3 minutes until smooth and thickened.

Remove from the heat and stir in the butter and lime zest. Allow to cool slightly, then add the egg yolks and beat well. Pour the mixture into the prepared flan case and bake for 15 minutes.

Meanwhile, make the topping: put the egg whites in a large bowl with the salt. Whisk until stiff, then add half the sugar. Continue whisking until standing in stiff peaks. Add the remaining sugar and whisk again.

Pile the meringue over the partly cooked flan, swirling the surface into peaks. Return to the oven for a further 15 minutes, until the peaks of the meringue are golden brown. Serve warm or cold.

PECAN PIE

SERVES 6

FOR THE PASTRY
115 g/4 oz butter, diced, plus more for greasing
225 g/8 oz flour
pinch of salt
3-4 tbsp iced water
lightly whipped cream or vanilla ice-cream, to serve
FOR THE FILLING
170 g/6 oz pecan halves
115 g/4 oz unsalted butter
115 g/4 oz soft light brown sugar
3½ tbsp double cream
30 g/1 oz flour, sifted

Preheat the oven to 190C/375F/gas5 and grease a 20 cm/8 in flan ring or loose-bottomed tart tin with butter.

Make the pastry: sieve the flour and salt into a mixing bowl. Lightly rub in the butter. Using a palette knife, mix in just enough iced water, a tablespoon at a time, to form a firm dough.

Knead lightly on a floured surface and use to line the prepared ring or tin. Prick the base and chill for at least 15 minutes.

Fill the flan case with baking beans and bake blind for 10 minutes. Remove the beans and return to the oven for a further 5 minutes to cook the base.

Meanwhile, prepare the filling: set aside 55 g/2 oz of the pecans and roughly chop the rest. Melt the butter with the sugar in a pan over a moderate heat, stirring, and bring to the boil. Beat in the cream and flour. Stir in the chopped nuts and bring back to the boil.

Spoon into the case and arrange the reserved pecan halves on top. Bake for 20 minutes until firm.

Serve warm or cold, accompanied by lightly whipped cream or vanilla ice-cream.

Top: Pecan Pie; bottom: Key Lime Pie

AUTUMN PUDDING

SERVES 6

2 dessert apples
1 firm pear
2 tbsp lemon juice
350 g/12 oz Victoria plums, stoned and quartered
350 g/12 oz greengages, halved and stoned
115 g/4 oz caster or golden granulated sugar
200 ml/7 fl oz sweet Muscatel wine
1 cinnamon stalk, halved
3 pieces of stem ginger in syrup, drained
and diced (optional)
10 large slices of white bread, crusts removed
double cream, to serve

Peel, core and chop the apples and the pear. Put the chopped fruit in a bowl and add the lemon juice. Mix well to prevent the fruit from discolouring.

Put all the fruit in a saucepan with the sugar, wine, cinnamon stick and ginger, if using. Bring to the boil, stirring frequently, then lower the heat and simmer for 15 minutes.

Use 8 slices of the bread to line the base and sides of a 1.75 litre/3 pt pudding basin. Spoon a few tablespoons of the fruit juices over the bread to moisten it and hold it in place, then spoon in the fruit and the rest of the juices.

Use the remaining bread to cover the fruit. Cover the basin with greaseproof paper and a weighted plate. Chill for a least 4 hours or overnight.

Unmould the pudding on a serving plate. Serve with double cream, plain or softly whipped.

Autumn Pudding

APPLE AND BERRY CRUMBLE

450 g/1 lb tart green apples, such as Bramleys
225 g/8 oz blackberries or loganberries
85 g/3 oz caster sugar
½ tsp ground cinnamon
butter, for greasing
cream or custard, to serve
FOR THE CRUMBLE TOPPING
170 g/6 oz flour
85 g/3 oz butter, diced
55 g/2 oz demerara sugar
1 tsp grated zest from an unwaxed lemon

Preheat the oven to 180C/350F/gas4 and grease a baking dish with butter.

First prepare the topping: sieve the flour into a mixing bowl and rub in the butter until the mixture resembles fine breadcrumbs. Stir in the sugar and lemon zest and set aside.

Peel, halve, core and thinly slice the apples. Place the slices in a bowl with the berries, sugar and cinnamon and toss lightly to mix.

Transfer the mixture to the prepared dish and sprinkle over the crumble mixture to cover completely.

Bake in the oven for about 35 minutes, until the top is golden brown. Serve hot with cream or custard.

The APPLE AND BERRY CRUMBLE lends itself to a wide range of variations. Try replacing the berries with sliced nectarines, peaches, plums, rhubarb or even raisins.

RHUBARB AND GOOSEBERRY COBBLER

450 g/1 lb rhubarb, cut into 2.5 cm/1 in chunks
225 g/8 oz fresh or frozen gooseberries
55 g/2 oz soft light brown sugar
1 bay leaf
butter, for greasing
pouring or clotted cream, to serve
FOR THE SCONE TOPPING
170 g/6 oz self-raising flour
pinch of salt
45 g/1½ oz butter
30 g/1 oz caster sugar
about 100 ml/3½ fl oz milk, plus extra for glazing
1 tbsp demerara sugar, for sprinkling

Preheat the oven to 220C/425F/gas7 and lightly grease a shallow 1.5 litre/2½ pt baking dish with butter.

Put the fruits in a saucepan with the sugar and bay leaf. Cook over a moderate heat, stirring frequently, for 12-15 minutes, until the fruit is almost tender.

Remove the bay leaf and spoon the fruit in an even layer into the base of the prepared baking dish.

Prepare the scone topping: sieve the flour and salt into a mixing bowl. Rub in the butter and stir in the sugar. Add the milk, mixing to form a firm dough.

Turn the dough out on a floured surface, knead lightly and roll out to a thickness of 1 cm/½ in. Using a 6 cm/2½ in pastry cutter, stamp out circles or shapes of pastry.

Arrange these on top of the fruit and brush with milk to glaze. Sprinkle the scones with the demerara sugar and bake in the oven for 15 minutes, until the cobbler topping is well risen and golden brown.

Serve hot, with pouring or clotted cream.

CHOCOLATE SPONGE PUDDINGS*

SERVES 6

85 g/3 oz butter, plus more for greasing
85 g/3 oz dark chocolate, cut into pieces
100 g/3½ oz caster sugar
2 eggs
(see page 2 for advice on eggs)*
5 tbsp sour cream
115 g/4 oz self-raising flour, sifted
icing sugar, for dusting
FOR THE BITTER CHOCOLATE SAUCE
100 g/3½ oz bitter dessert chocolate
30 g/1 oz butter
3 tbsp rum or brandy

Preheat the oven to 180C/350F/gas4. Grease 6 dariole or individual pudding moulds with butter and then line their bases with greaseproof paper.

Put the chocolate in a small saucepan with 125 ml/4 fl oz of water. Stir over a low heat until melted and smooth. Remove from the heat.

In a mixing bowl, beat the butter and sugar until light and fluffy. Beat in the eggs, one at a time. Stir in the prepared chocolate mixture then fold in alternating spoonfuls of the sour cream and flour.

Spoon the mixture between the prepared moulds. Place them on a baking sheet and bake in the oven for about 15 minutes, until just firm to the touch.

Meanwhile, prepare the sauce: put the chocolate and butter in a small saucepan with 3 tablespoons of water. Stir constantly over a gentle heat until smooth and melted. Stir in the rum or brandy.

Turn the puddings out on individual serving plates. Dredge with a little icing sugar and spoon the sauce over them to serve.

LEMON AND TREACLE PUDDING

115 g/4 oz butter, plus extra for greasing
115 g/4 oz caster sugar
finely grated zest of 2 unwaxed lemons
2 eggs, beaten
170 g/6 oz self-raising flour
4 tbsp golden syrup
cream or vanilla custard, to serve

Grease a 1.1 litre/2 pt pudding basin with butter and line the base with a disc of greaseproof paper.

Beat together the butter, sugar and lemon zest until light and fluffy. Beat in the eggs, a little at a time, and then fold in the flour.

Spoon the syrup into the bottom of the prepared basin. Spoon in the lemon sponge mixture.

Cover the basin with a layer of pleated greaseproof paper and with foil. Secure tightly with string. Place in a large pan and add enough water to come three-quarters up the basin. Cover tightly, bring to a simmer and steam the pudding for 1½-2 hours until firm, topping up the water occasionally.

Turn out on a serving plate and serve accompanied by cream or custard.

64

INDEX

Page numbers in *italic*
refer to the photographs

ACKNOWLEDGEMENTS
The Author would like to give special thanks to the following people: Jacqui Gibson for her help testing recipes and during photography, and particularly for her good-humoured support on location; Rick for his encouragement along the way to get the work done; and finally Lewis Esson for tracking her down, tactfully correcting mistakes and much more.